THE OFFICIAL

ANNUAL 2022

Written by **Richard Godden** and **Dominic Bliss**

Designed by **Daniel May**

A Grange Publication

© 2021. Published by Grange Communications Ltd., Edinburgh, under licence from
Chelsea FC Merchandising Limited. www.chelseafc.com. Printed in the EU.

ISBN 978-1-913578-70-1

CONTENTS

WELCOME TO THE OFFICIAL ANNUAL OF THE CHAMPIONS OF EUROPE!

The Chelsea FC Annual 2022 celebrates our incredible run to Champions League glory last season and, on top of that, we've got everything you need to know on our previous triumph in the competition as we celebrate the 10th anniversary of that incredible campaign. Remember, we're still London's first, and only, Champions League winners!

There's plenty more packed into this year's Annual, as we take you deep inside the club with an extensive look at our men's squad and all you need to know about the Academy and Women's sides who also wear the blue shirt with pride. We've also got Q&As with some of the key players who feature for those teams.

It's not all about the here and now, either, as we focus on one of the club's most charismatic managers from yesteryear and remind you of some of the players who have given incredible service to the club, as club captain Cesar Azpilicueta celebrates a decade in west London.

There are also loads of quizzes and games for you to show off your Chelsea knowledge – and we've got a signed home shirt up for grabs for one lucky reader!

Keep the blue flag flying high, and remember – win or lose, up the Blues!

Stamford and Bridget

WE'VE DONE IT AGAIN!

How good does it feel to become a European champion? Just look at the joy etched across the faces of our players, as Chelsea joined an elite group of clubs to have won the Champions League twice, following our 1-0 win over Manchester City in the 2020/21 final.

CHAMPIONS OF EUROPE!

A season full of ups and downs ultimately ended on the biggest high of the lot with Chelsea being crowned Champions League winners for the second time in our history. It was a campaign that seemed to have it all, so let's try and recap a quite astonishing eight months, most of which played out in front of empty stadiums...

Reece James got us off to a flier when he netted a Goal of the Season contender in our first match of 2020/21, as he belted one in against Brighton. However, it was an up and down start to the campaign, despite our prolific form in front of goal, as we recorded two 3-3 draws in our first five matches, including coming from 3-0 down against West Brom.

Our form in the Champions League was superb, though, as we cruised through Group E with the minimum of fuss. New goalkeeper Edouard Mendy conceded only twice, one of which came against his old club Rennes, as we took full points from four of the first five games, and our qualification was secured with a thumping 4-0 win at the home of perennial Europa League winners Sevilla. Olivier Giroud scored all four goals, the first three of which were a perfect hat-trick (scoring goals with both feet and a header).

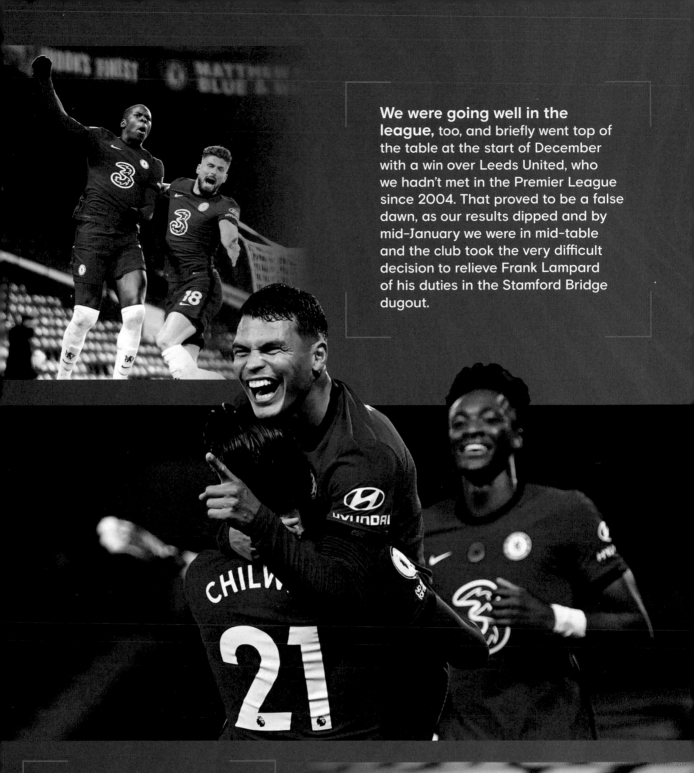

We were going well in the league, too, and briefly went top of the table at the start of December with a win over Leeds United, who we hadn't met in the Premier League since 2004. That proved to be a false dawn, as our results dipped and by mid-January we were in mid-table and the club took the very difficult decision to relieve Frank Lampard of his duties in the Stamford Bridge dugout.

Thomas Tuchel was appointed in his place, and the German head coach immediately set about tightening up our defence. Teams suddenly found no way past our three-man rearguard and Mendy was going through matches without having a save to make! Beating Tottenham 1-0, thanks to a Jorginho penalty, was the highlight of Tuchel's early weeks in the job.

The Champions League knockout stages were soon upon us, and a spectacular overhead kick from Giroud helped see off Atletico Madrid in the away leg of arguably the toughest tie of the last 16. Hakim Ziyech and Emerson finished the job off at the Bridge to see us through.

We continued to go well domestically, with vital wins over the two Merseyside clubs, but all eyes were on Europe as we started to dream of going all the way. Brilliant goals from Mason Mount and Ben Chilwell got us past Porto in a strange tie where both legs were played at Sevilla's stadium due to Covid-19 related travel restrictions.

The business end of the season was upon us, and there could hardly have been more at stake. After beating Manchester City to earn a spot in the FA Cup final for the second straight season, there was the small matter of a Champions League semi-final against the mighty Real Madrid. Incredibly, it was the first time we'd met them in the competition, but we were brilliant across the two legs, as goals from Christian Pulisic, Timo Werner and Mason Mount saw us into our third Champions League final!

Unfortunately, the FA Cup final didn't go to plan, as we were beaten by Leicester City, who clinched the trophy for the first time in their history. To be fair, the winning goal by Youri Tielemans was pretty special, but we got our revenge in the very next game by beating them at the Bridge, which helped seal fourth place in the Premier League.

All that was left to play for was the small matter of the Champions League trophy, as we met Manchester City in an all-English final played in Porto. Some pundits had the Blues as underdogs, but we produced a performance for the ages! N'Golo Kante led the way with his third consecutive Man of the Match display in Europe, but every player was magnificent in nullifying a free-scoring City side. Of course, all the headlines went to Kai Havertz, though, as our summer signing from Bayer Leverkusen repaid every penny of his transfer fee with a brilliant winning goal. That it was played in front of fans made it all the sweeter, as we were crowned champions of Europe for the second time.

TUCHEL
TAKES THE REINS

Thomas Tuchel took his place in the Stamford Bridge dugout in January 2021 and guided us to Champions League glory in his first half-season in charge. Here's everything you need to know about Chelsea's first German head coach...

HUMBLE BEGINNINGS

Thomas Tuchel was born in Bavaria, the same region in Germany where Chelsea won the Champions League in 2012. He is from a small town called Krumbach and as a young footballer, he played as a centre-back.

He played for Augsburg as a youth player, and then became a professional with two lower league teams in Germany – Stuttgarter Kickers and SSV Ulm.

Sadly, a bad injury forced Tuchel to retire from playing when he was 25 years old, so he decided to become a coach.

He started out working as an academy coach with several German clubs, and when his Mainz team won the Under-19s championship in the 2008/09 season, he was promoted to take charge of the first team. You've probably heard of the guy he replaced – it was Jurgen Klopp!

STEPS UP

Mainz were new to the top division in Germany (the Bundesliga) when Tuchel took over, but he turned them into a top team during his five years there. They seemed to get better every year, gradually moving into the top half and eventually qualifying for the Europa League, thanks to Tuchel's smart tactics.

His work with Mainz earned him a big job in 2014, when Borussia Dortmund named him as their new boss. It was the second time that Tuchel had replaced Klopp, who left Dortmund after a seventh-place finish in his last season.

CUP CONQUEST

Dortmund recovered to finish second and third in the league in their two seasons under Tuchel. They also did well in Europe, reaching the quarter-finals of the Europa League and the Champions League. That was Tuchel's first taste of the Champions League, and he also got his first taste of winning a major trophy with Dortmund in 2017, when they won the German Cup, which is called the DFB-Pokal.

PRIZES IN PARIS

Now that he was a cup winner and a Champions League coach, Tuchel was becoming well known abroad as well, and in 2018 he moved to Paris Saint-Germain, or PSG as they are better known.

He took charge of some of the biggest names in football at PSG, with Neymar and Kylian Mbappe among the players he worked with in the French capital.

Tuchel was hungry for success and he won trophy after trophy in Paris. In two-and-a-half years in charge of the club, he won two league titles, the French Cup and the French League Cup. He also reached the Champions League final in 2020, when PSG lost out to the same Bayern Munich team that knocked out Chelsea earlier in the competition.

BLUES BROTHERS

One of Tuchel's most important players at PSG was Thiago Silva, who joined Chelsea after that Champions League final defeat in the summer of 2020.

Tuchel and Silva made a great team – they won every trophy in French football together and now they have brought their hunger for success to Stamford Bridge, where we love nothing more than winning trophies.

Before that, Tuchel also worked with another Chelsea

star, when he gave a 17-year-old Christian Pulisic his senior debut for Borussia Dortmund in January 2016.

CHAMPIONS OF EUROPE

Tuchel arrived at Chelsea in January 2021, and it was the first time that he had started a new job in the middle of a season.

Frank Lampard had already guided us through the Champions League group stage when he left the club, and Tuchel continued our European run in style. With him in charge, we beat Atletico Madrid, Porto and Real Madrid on the way to a final against Manchester City.

It was a great final, played in Porto's stadium, the Estadio do Dragao, and Chelsea ran out 1-0 winners thanks to Kai Havertz's brilliant goal. Tuchel had his first trophy with Chelsea – and it was the biggest one of all!

When Tuchel arrived at Stamford Bridge, we were 10th in the Premier League and had played exactly half of our games, but his organised system helped us to become stronger defensively and we built from this base to improve our results in the second half of the season.

Chelsea finished the season in fourth place as it turned out to be a year to remember for Blues supporters...and for Thomas Tuchel!

TUCHEL'S TROPHIES

Borussia Dortmund
German Cup 2016/17

Paris Saint-Germain
Ligue 1 2018/19, 2019/20
French Cup 2019/20
French League Cup 2019/20
Trophee des Champions 2018, 2019

Chelsea
Champions League 2020/21
UEFA Super Cup 2021

PLAYER PROFILES

*All stats correct ahead of the 2021/22 season

Kepa **ARRIZABALAGA**

Position: Goalkeeper
Date of birth: 03. 10. 1994
Nationality: Spanish
Signed from: Athletic Bilbao (August 2018)
Chelsea appearances: 109
Clean sheets: 39

Did you know?

Kepa saved two penalties in the shootout at the end of our Europa League semi-final against Eintracht Frankfurt in 2018/19, and we went on to win the trophy.

Marcus **BETTINELLI**

Position: Goalkeeper
Date of birth: 24. 05. 1992
Nationality: English
Signed from: Fulham (July 2021)
Chelsea appearances: 0
Clean sheets: 0

Did you know?

Bettinelli was in goal for Fulham when they won the Championship Play-Off final against Aston Villa at Wembley in 2018.

Edouard **MENDY**

Position: Goalkeeper
Date of birth: 01 .03. 1992
Nationality: Senegalese
Signed from: Rennes (September 2020)
Chelsea appearances: 44
Clean sheets: 25

Did you know?

Mendy joined Chelsea from Rennes, the same French team we signed arguably our greatest-ever goalkeeper Petr Cech from back in 2004.

Marcos **ALONSO**

Position: Defender
Date of birth: 28. 12. 1990
Nationality: Spanish
Signed from: Fiorentina (August 2016)
Chelsea appearances: 166
Goals: 24

Did you know?

Alonso loves golf and used to represent Madrid when he was a kid. One of his dad's friends growing up was Seve Ballesteros, one of the greatest golfers of all time!

Cesar **AZPILICUETA**

Position: Defender
Date of birth: 28. 08. 1989
Nationality: Spanish
Signed from: Marseille (August 2012)
Chelsea appearances: 429
Goals: 14

Did you know?

Azpilicueta's home town is Pamplona, where they let bulls loose in the streets once a year for a summer festival known as "the running of the bulls"!

Trevoh **CHALOBAH**

Position: Defender
Date of birth: 05. 07. 1999
Nationality: English
Signed from: Chelsea Academy (July 2016)
Chelsea appearances: 0
Goals: 0

Did you know?

Trevoh's older brother Nathaniel came through the ranks at Chelsea too and made 15 first-team appearances for the club. He now plays for Watford.

Ben C**HILWELL**

Position: Defender
Date of birth: 21. 12. 1996
Nationality: English
Signed from: Leicester City (August 2020)
Chelsea appearances: 42
Goals: 4

Did you know?

Chilwell was a bit of a sporting all-rounder as a schoolboy. He represented his county at both cross-country running and cricket before deciding to focus on football as a teenager.

Andreas **CHRISTENSEN**

Position: Defender
Date of birth: 10. 04. 1996
Nationality: Danish
Signed from: Chelsea Academy (July 2013)
Chelsea appearances: 127
Goals: 0

Did you know?

Christensen's dad, Sten, used to be a goalkeeper for one of the biggest teams in Denmark, Brondby, and was one of Andreas' first coaches too.

Reece JAMES

Position: Defender
Date of birth: 08. 12. 1999
Nationality: English
Signed from: Chelsea Academy
(March 2017)
Chelsea appearances: 84
Goals: 3

Did you know?
James' sister Lauren is a top player as well, and joined Chelsea Women from Manchester United in the summer.

Antonio RUDIGER

Position: Defender
Date of birth: 03. 03. 1993
Nationality: German
Signed from: Roma (July 2017)
Chelsea appearances: 149
Goals: 7

Did you know?
Rudiger has four sisters and one brother, called Sahr Senesie, who used to be a professional footballer as well and is now Antonio's agent.

Thiago SILVA

Position: Defender
Date of birth: 22. 09. 1984
Nationality: Brazilian
Signed from: Paris Saint-Germain
(August 2020)
Chelsea appearances: 34
Goals: 2

Did you know?
Thiago Silva once scored against Chelsea at Stamford Bridge, when he was a Paris Saint-Germain player, in the Champions League last 16 in March 2015.

Kai HAVERTZ

Position: Midfielder
Date of birth: 11. 06. 1999
Nationality: German
Signed from: Bayer Leverkusen
(September 2020)
Chelsea appearances: 45
Goals: 9

Did you know?
The top division in German football is called the Bundesliga, and Havertz became the youngest player ever to play 100 games in it, at the age of 20 years, six months and four days. The previous record holder had been Timo Werner!

Callum HUDSON-ODOI

Position: Midfielder
Date of birth: 07. 11. 2000
Nationality: English
Signed from: Chelsea Academy
(November 2017)
Chelsea appearances: 98
Goals: 13

Did you know?
Hudson-Odoi's dad, whose name is Bismark, was also a professional footballer, playing for a club called Hearts of Oak, in Ghana.

JORGINHO

Position: Midfielder
Date of birth: 20. 12. 1991
Nationality: Italian
Signed from: Napoli (July 2018)
Chelsea appearances: 141
Goals: 17

Did you know?
Although he plays for the Italian national team, Jorginho was born and raised in Brazil, and moved to Italy at the age of 15.

N'Golo KANTE

Position: Midfielder
Date of birth: 29. 03. 1991
Nationality: French
Signed from: Leicester City (July 2016)
Chelsea appearances: 218
Goals: 11

Did you know?
Kante was turned down by every academy he trialled for, and only became a footballer by joining a sixth division team in France at the age of 19.

Mateo KOVACIC

Position: Midfielder
Date of birth: 06. 05. 1994
Nationality: Croatian
Signed from: Real Madrid (July 2019)
Chelsea appearances: 140
Goals: 2

Did you know?
Kovacic was born and raised in Linz, in Austria, which is the geographical centre of Europe.

Ruben **LOFTUS-CHEEK**

Position: Midfielder
Date of birth: 23. 01. 1996
Nationality: English
Signed from: Chelsea Academy
(January 2013)
Chelsea appearances: 82
Goals: 12

Did you know?

Loftus-Cheek was part of the England squad that reached the World Cup semi-finals in 2018, making four appearances in Russia under Gareth Southgate.

Mason **MOUNT**

Position: Midfielder
Date of birth: 10. 01. 1999
Nationality: English
Signed from: Chelsea Academy
(January 2016)
Chelsea appearances: 107
Goals: 17

Did you know?

Mount's grand-dad, Bill, was a boxer and he says he can see the same fighting spirit in Mason when he plays football.

Saul **NIGUEZ**

Position: Midfielder
Date of birth: 21. 11. 1994
Nationality: Spanish
Signed from: Atletico Madrid (August 2021)
Chelsea appearances: 0
Goals: 0

Did you know?

Saul played against Chelsea in both legs of last season's Champions League last 16 tie, when he was with Atletico Madrid.

Christian **PULISIC**

Position: Midfielder/Forward
Date of birth: 18. 09. 1998
Nationality: American
Signed from: Borussia Dortmund
(January 2019)
Chelsea appearances: 77
Goals: 17

Did you know?

Pulisic grew up in Hershey, Pennsylvania, where there is a world-famous chocolate factory. He told us the air smells of Reese's Peanut Butter Cup when it rains!

Hakim **ZIYECH**

Position: Midfielder/Forward
Date of birth: 19. 03. 1993
Nationality: Moroccan
Signed from: Ajax (July 2020)
Chelsea appearances: 39
Goals: 6

Did you know?

Ziyech grew up in the Netherlands and represented the country of his birth up until Under-21s level, before deciding to play senior international football for his ancestral home, Morocco.

Romelu **LUKAKU**

Position: Forward
Date of birth: 13. 05. 1993
Nationality: Belgian
Signed from: Inter Milan (August 2021)
Chelsea appearances: 15
Goals: 0

Did you know?

Lukaku was named the Most Valuable Player (MVP) in the Italian Serie A last season, after scoring 24 goals and registering 11 assists as Inter won the title.

Timo **WERNER**

Position: Forward
Date of birth: 06. 03. 1996
Nationality: German
Signed from: RB Leipzig (July 2020)
Chelsea appearances: 52
Goals: 12

Did you know?

Werner won the Golden Boot at the 2017 FIFA Confederations Cup when he was just 21 years old, as Germany won the summer competition.

CHELSEA MEN'S QUIZ

1 Mateo Kovacic plays international football for Croatia, but in which country was he born?

  ◯ a) Austria   ◯ b) Australia   ◯ c) Italy

2 Which two Chelsea players won both the Champions League and the European Championships in 2021, making it a successful year for club and country?

  [   ]   [   ]

3 True or False: Edouard Mendy plays international football for Cameroon.

  ◯ True   ◯ False

4 At which German club did Thomas Tuchel give a 17-year-old Christian Pulisic his senior debut in 2016?

  ◯ a) Bayern Munich   ◯ b) Borussia Dortmund   ◯ c) Bayer Leverkusen

5 Thiago Silva reached the Champions League final in both of the last two seasons. He won it with Chelsea in 2021, but which club was he playing for when he received a runners-up medal in the 2020 final?

  ◯ a) Barcelona   ◯ b) PSG   ◯ c) Ajax

6 Which two players finished as Chelsea's joint top scorers in all competitions in the 2020/21 season, with 12 goals?

  [   ]   [   ]

7 True or False: Reece James had a loan spell with Wigan Athletic before making his first-team debut for Chelsea.

  ◯ True   ◯ False

8 Who played the pass to assist Kai Havertz for his winning goal against Manchester City in last season's Champions League final?

  ◯ a) N'Golo Kante   ◯ b) Jorginho   ◯ c) Mason Mount

9 N'Golo Kante has won the Premier League with two different clubs. One is Chelsea, but with which other club did he top the table?

  [   ]

10 Which Chelsea player was the top-scoring defender in the Premier League in the 2020/21 season?

  [   ]

CHELSEA WOMEN'S QUIZ

1 Fran Kirby is our all-time leading goalscorer, but which legendary former Blues striker's tally did she overhaul?

- a) Eniola Aluko
- b) Gemma Davison
- c) Karen Carney

2 Which country "Down Under" does Sam Kerr come from?

- a) Australia
- b) New Zealand
- c) Papua New Guinea

3 Which Chelsea player won Olympic Gold with her nation in the Tokyo Games?

- a) Jessie Fleming
- b) Magdalena Eriksson
- c) Sam Kerr

4 From which club, who also wear blue, did Chelsea sign goalkeeper Ann-Katrin Berger?

- a) Brighton & Hove Albion
- b) Birmingham City
- c) Everton

5 Which number does Ji So-Yun wear for the Blues?

- a) 7
- b) 10
- c) 11

6 Who was named captain in 2019 after Karen Carney's retirement?

- a) Magdalena Eriksson
- b) Sophie Ingle
- c) Carly Telford

7 Sam Kerr was our top scorer in the 2020/21 season, but who took that honour in the previous two campaigns?

- a) Erin Cuthbert
- b) Bethany England
- c) Fran Kirby

8 Which Scandinavian player joined Chelsea for a world-record fee in the summer of 2020?

- u) Jonna Andersson
- b) Pernille Harder
- c) Guro Reiten

9 Chelsea's regular back four in the 2020/21 season was made up by Jonna Andersson, Millie Bright, Magdalena Eriksson and which other player?

- a) Jess Carter
- b) Niamh Charles
- c) Maren Mjelde

10 After signing for Chelsea, which player admitted that one of her hobbies was to paint pictures of monkeys?!

- a) Guro Reiten
- b) Melanie Leupolz
- c) Zecira Musovic

Answers on p63

23

ROMELU!

This summer, Romelu Lukaku returned to Stamford Bridge, a decade after he first joined Chelsea as a teenage talent back in 2011. Now 28, and one of the top strikers in world football, he's back with the Blues...

BLUE THROUGH AND THROUGH

Romelu Lukaku was a Chelsea supporter as a boy and grew up dreaming of playing at Stamford Bridge. He was filmed on a stadium tour as a schoolboy, when he insisted that he would one day play on the hallowed turf, and he got his chance when we signed him from Belgian club Anderlecht as an 18-year-old in 2011. He made his first debut here in August 2011, when he came off the bench in a Premier League game against Norwich City (pictured). Now he is back and he is hungry for success this time around.

"The relationship I have with this club means so much to me," he said when he signed for us for a second time this summer. "I have supported Chelsea as a kid and now to be back and try to help them win more titles is an amazing feeling."

GOALS, GOALS, GOALS

A lot has happened in the 10 years since Lukaku first walked through the doors here. While he was a Chelsea player the first time around, he had successful loan spells with West Bromwich Albion and Everton, who he joined on a permanent basis in 2014. He became Everton's all-time leading Premier League goalscorer over the course of his time there, and his incredible goalscoring form at Goodison Park earned him a move to Manchester United in 2017. He spent two seasons at Old Trafford – finishing as United's top scorer in 2017/18 – before moving to Italy to play for Inter Milan, where the goals continued to flow. Lukaku is also the all-time top scorer for the Belgium national team, with 64 international goals to his name in 98 caps at the time this annual was printed.

ROMELU'S RETURN

Lukaku has become one of the best goalscorers in the game and has re-joined us at his peak. He won the Italian league title with Inter last season, under the management of former Blues boss Antonio Conte, and scored 64 goals in his two seasons there. He was also named in the Team of the Tournament for Euro 2020, after starring for Belgium in the summer competition. When he was unveiled as a Chelsea player once again in August, his determination to succeed here was clear for everyone to see.

"I'm happy and blessed to be back at this wonderful club," he said. "It's been a long journey for me: I came here as a kid who had a lot to learn, now I'm coming back with a lot of experience and more mature.

"Since I left Chelsea, it's been a long journey with a lot of ups and downs, but these experiences made me strong and the challenge is to try to help the team win some more trophies."

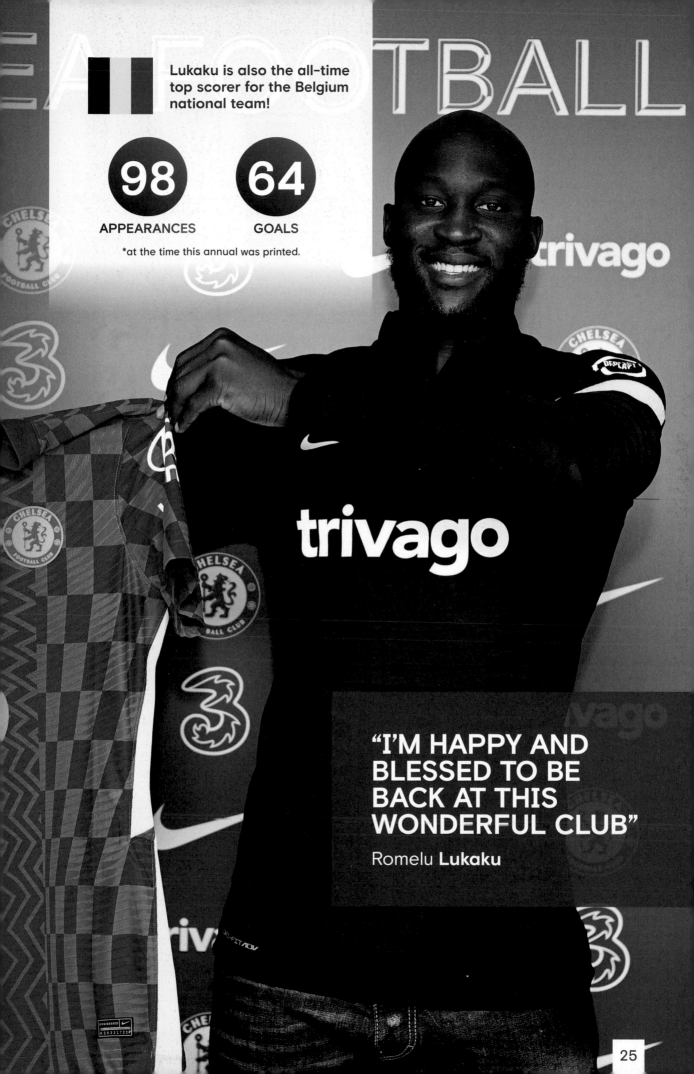

Lukaku is also the all-time top scorer for the Belgium national team!

98 APPEARANCES

64 GOALS

*at the time this annual was printed.

trivago

"I'M HAPPY AND BLESSED TO BE BACK AT THIS WONDERFUL CLUB"

Romelu **Lukaku**

MASON'S MAGIC

Our Player of the Year for the 2020/21 season was Mason Mount, our midfield marvel who is Chelsea through and through. He ended a campaign to remember with his first piece of silverware…and it was the biggest prize of all!

Any player that comes through the Academy to become a first-team regular can expect to become a fans' favourite at Stamford Bridge. The Chelsea supporters love to cheer for one of their own youth products, and Mason Mount has been with the club since he was an eight-year-old and worked his way through the age groups to become a senior professional.

In 2019/20, he became the first youth-team graduate to make 50 appearances in the same season he made his senior debut, and he followed that up by moving to another level in 2020/21, as he won the Chelsea Player of the Year award in a Champions League-winning campaign.

With nine goals in 48 games across all competitions, he scored one more than he

had done the previous year, and he certainly managed some important ones, scoring against Porto in the quarter-finals of the Champions League, before bagging the goal that sealed victory in the semi-final against Real Madrid.

How did it feel to be named Chelsea Player of the Year?

Following in the footsteps of some legends from this club, it means a lot to me. It's been special for me to come through this long journey that I've been on and to now be in the first team. The support and appreciation I get from the fans really means a lot to me

and gives me a lot of confidence every time I step out on the pitch. When I was presented with the award before the Leicester match late last season, it was a special day for me to have the fans back at the Bridge that night, and my family there as well.

Who have been the most important people in helping you reach this level?

I want to say thanks to the Academy, all the coaches I worked under, Jim Fraser, Neil Bath. This is for them as well. Without the Academy, I wouldn't be sitting here now, so for me to win this Player of the Year award, I give it to them. It's down to them that I've got here. It's been a crazy journey and they've lived with me through it. I owe a lot to them, to the coaches that I've worked under.

What was it like to play in the Champions League final and win it?

A Champions League final is different to most other games you play in. You don't get to experience it very often and some players even with long careers in the game never get the opportunity to be involved in one.

It's a special occasion and to win it was a dream come true for all of us because everybody stepped up. It was an up and down season where we found ourselves mid-table halfway through but to win it was unbelievable. That wasn't just an individual effort or a few players, it was the whole team and we really came together.

Do you set yourself goals to keep improving?

You have to set goals before every season and you have to really set the target high to want to achieve that. I always want to go for 10 goals and just came short of that last season but I had a lot chances so I couldn't look at it and say I was happy with nine. I could and should have had way more, which is something that I'll definitely be looking at.

I was speaking to Joe Edwards [assistant coach] recently about where on the pitch I am most productive and I actually score most of my goals from the middle of the box. So, where there are areas that I can do better, I need to look at them and see what I can improve on.

FINAL 2021
PORTO

THE ACADEMY

DEVELOPMENT SQUAD

Chelsea's Under-23s team is known as the development squad, and both their coach and his assistant coach, Andy Myers and Jon Harley, played for Chelsea when they were younger.

After winning the league in 2019/20, they finished second in 2020/21, behind Manchester City, and Myers was pleased with the hard work everyone put in during a difficult time.

Andy Myers and Jon Harley

"It's been a very good campaign all-round," he said at the end of the season. "The boys have done well, and I have to say a massive thank you to the club for the way they've handled things for the Academy during this pandemic. I also want to thank the staff I work with as well, who have done a really good job."

UNDER-18s

Our Under-18s finished seventh in their league, and also competed in two FA Youth Cup competitions. The reason for this was the Covid-19 pandemic, which delayed the end of the Youth Cup from 2019/20.

Jude Soonsup-Bell

In the end, the semi-finals and finals were played in autumn of last season, and Chelsea beat Manchester United to reach the final, where we lost 3-2 to Manchester City. We then reached the fifth round of the 2020/21 FA Youth Cup, but were beaten 2-1 by Everton.

Jude Soonsup-Bell finished as the Under-18s' top scorer, with 18 goals, and he also scored one for the development squad, making it 19 in total for the teenage striker.

Trevoh Chalobah

ACADEMY GRADUATES ACHIEVE A CENTURY

During the 2020/21 season, Chelsea completed a 100-game run in which at least one graduate from our Academy had appeared in the starting line-up for the first team. The run began with our Europa League semi-final first leg against Eintracht Frankfurt on 2 May 2019, when both Andreas Christensen and Ruben Loftus-Cheek (pictured) started in Germany. It then continued all the way through to our Premier League game against Everton on 8 March 2021, when Christensen once again started, alongside Reece James on this occasion.

In every game along the way, there was at least one of the club's own youth products on the pitch for Chelsea when the match kicked off. After that match against Everton, the run continued for every fixture until the end of the 2020/21 season, and was still going strong at the outset of the current campaign as Trevoh Chalobah joined the Academy graduates to have started for the first team during that period. After scoring in our opening Premier League game of the 2021/22 season, he was congratulated by his old Academy team-mate, Mason Mount.

Ruben Loftus-Cheek

A DECADE OF

AZ PI

This season is Cesar Azpilicueta's 10th campaign with Chelsea, so it seems like the right time to take a look back at the Blues skipper's sensational stint at Stamford Bridge, at the end of a year when he finally got his hands on the biggest prize of all!

THE MAKING OF A LEGEND

Cesar Azpilicueta joined Chelsea in the summer of 2012, just after we had been crowned Champions League winners for the first time in our history. At that time, he was known as an exciting right-back who had shown great potential during his time with French club Marseille and, before that, with his home-town club Osasuna, in Spain.

He admits his life has changed quite a lot since he first arrived in London just before his 23rd birthday.

"It has gone so quick!" he said. "My personal life has changed quite a lot here – I arrived here with just my wife and now we have three kids who have grown up here. They speak better English than Spanish, and sometimes they correct my English!

"As a footballer, I'm not the same now as when I arrived. I have lots more experience – I arrived as a really young man, and now I'm in my thirties, so obviously a lot happens in that time."

MR VERSATILE

Azpi has been popular with every manager he has played for, and part of the reason for that is his willingness to play in several different positions. He arrived as a right-back in 2012, played as a left-back as we won the Premier League in 2014/15, and was on the right side of a back three when we won it again in 2016/17. Under Thomas Tuchel, he has played as a right wing-back and one of the three centre-backs in our usual 3-4-3 system. Talk about versatile!

"I feel really proud every time I put the Chelsea shirt on"

TAKING THE ARMBAND

When Gary Cahill left the club in 2019, Chelsea needed a new captain, and there was one obvious candidate for the job – Cesar Azpilicueta. He had already worn the armband for plenty of matches when Cahill or John Terry were not in the team, but in 2019/20 he became the official men's team captain.

Being skipper isn't just about leading the team out, though. You also have to organise the players on the pitch, give instructions to your team-mates, help the less experienced players to settle in and make sure you think of everyone in the dressing room. Azpi understands this all very well.

"My goal is always to get the maximum out of everybody," he explained. "Whenever I feel someone needs it, I will always be there to help."

FANS' FAVOURITE

With more than 400 Chelsea games under his belt now, Azpilicueta is eighth in the list of players to have made most appearances for the club in our history. The only overseas player ahead of him on the list is legendary goalkeeper Petr Cech.

It's no surprise that the supporters have grown to love him. From the moment he arrived, they were singing his name – well, not quite! Some of the fans found his name difficult to pronounce, so they jokingly nicknamed him 'Dave', but it was just a bit of fun and now they sing his full name as part of his chant: "Az-pil-i-cue-ta, we'll just call him Dave!"

A banner in his honour appeared in the stands halfway through last season, located between the East Stand and the Matthew Harding Stand. "I'm very grateful for that," he said. "It's very nice to see your name there, with so many legends around. I have had a strong connection with the fans since I arrived in here in 2012 and to have this connection is something special – I feel really proud every time I put the Chelsea shirt on."

SHOW US YOUR MEDALS!

No profile of Azpi would be complete without talking about his incredible medals collection. Let's take a look at the trophies he has lifted in his time with Chelsea.

He won the Europa League at the end of his first season here, then picked up League Cup and Premier League winner's medals in 2014/15, before winning the league again two years later. In 2017/18, he completed his set of major domestic honours when we won the FA Cup at Wembley, then a year later he added a second Europa League triumph to the list.

The biggest moment of all came in Porto last May, though, when he lifted the Champions League trophy as captain. Not many players can say they've done that.

LEADING THE WAY

Cesar Azpilicueta broke into the top 10 leading appearance-makers for the Blues last term, which puts him in esteemed company. Here's a little bit about the men who have played more games for Chelsea than anyone else...

Ron **Harris**

795 Appearances

This is a record that won't be broken in a hurry! The man who was known in English football as Chopper – just ask any opposition centre-forward on the receiving end of a Harris tackle – made his Chelsea debut in 1962 and he was still playing for us 18 years later! In that time, he became the first skipper to lift the FA Cup and a European trophy, and he was captain for almost half of his club-record tally of appearances as a Blue.

Peter **Bonetti**

729 Appearances

Next on the list is another former Blue with an excellent nickname. The Cat was agile and blessed with razor-sharp reflexes, which made him a fans' favourite throughout his two decades at the club in the 1960s and '70s. He was even a pioneer off the pitch, as he brought out his own range of gloves – which were green, to match his goalkeeper kit – and he long held the club record for clean sheets until it was surpassed by Petr Cech.

John **Terry**

717 Appearances

Chelsea's captain, leader, legend is the only other player to have passed 700 appearances for the club. When you consider only 492 of those were in the Premier League, it just goes to show how successful we were in numerous competitions during his time here, as JT won the lot. Not only was he a rock-solid centre-back, he also holds the record for most goals by a defender for Chelsea, which simply added to his legend status.

Frank **Lampard**

648 Appearances

Whether it is the title-decider in Bolton, his spinning half-volley against Bayern at the Bridge, his cheeky chip from the tightest of angles in the Nou Camp, or any number of crucial contributions he has made to our recent success, every supporter will have their own favourite Lampard moment. After 13 years, 648 appearances and a club-record 211 goals, Lampard departed Chelsea in the summer of 2014 as perhaps the greatest player to have pulled on the blue shirt.

John **Hollins**

592 Appearances

Chelsea fans loved this energetic midfielder, who matched endurance with durability by rarely missing a game. Twice he was voted our Player of the Year, and it came in our two trophy-winning campaigns in the 1970s, which shows just how important he was to the team. His appearance total came from two separate spells at the club, the second of which came in the 1980s, and he also had a stint as our manager.

Petr **Cech**

494 Appearances

No overseas player has appeared in more games for the Blues than the goalkeeper known as Big Pete, although his tally may soon come under threat from Azpi. One thing he won't be giving up any time soon is his club-record haul of clean sheets, which stands at 228, and he also holds the Premier League record. Let's not forget his penalty-saving antics in Munich, which helped secure our first Champions League.

Dennis **Wise**

445 Appearances

Wise saw himself as a representative of Chelsea fans on the pitch, never giving less than 100 per cent for the badge. Sometimes he got into a bit of trouble, but let's not overlook the fact he had bundles of talent too, which made him a key man as we started winning trophies again in the late 1990s. Wise was the skipper for all those triumphs, and he helped welcome the new foreign contingent who were ushering in a new dawn in west London.

Cesar **Azpilicueta**

429 Appearances

Only the second man to have lifted the Champions League trophy as captain of Chelsea, Azpi has become a club legend in his near 10-year stay in west London. He came here as an attacking right-back, but his 429 appearances have come in a variety of different positions along the back-line – in fact, he's filled just about every defensive role possible for the club! He's also a lead-by-example captain who accepts nothing other than victory. *'Stat correct at beginning of 2021/22 season*

Steve **Clarke**

421 Appearances

You may have spotted Clarke in the Scotland dugout at Euro 2020, but before that he was a handy player for Chelsea, as consistent a defender as you can imagine. Having endured relegation and countless disappointments throughout his first 10 campaigns as a Blue – save for a Division Two title and Full Members Cup – Clarke was rewarded for his loyalty in his final two years as a player as we won three major honours.

Kerry **Dixon**

420 Appearances

Chelsea fans christened him King Kerry, as this centre-forward arrived in 1983 as a renowned scorer at a lower level and promptly won the Golden Boot in both Division Two and Division One! He was a key figure in our revival in the 1980s and by the time he departed, he was just nine goals shy of Bobby Tambling's club record, although he had played in 50 games more. In fact, he is the only striker to surpass the 400-appearance mark for Chelsea.

CHAMPIONS
OF EUROPE 2012

This season marks the 10th anniversary of our first Champions League triumph in 2012, when we beat Bayern Munich in their own stadium to lift the famous trophy after years of near misses. Didier Drogba and Petr Cech were the heroes on a night that nobody who was there will ever forget...

THE ROAD TO MUNICH

The 2011/12 season looked like it would be a disappointing one. Our league form was poor, and we ended up finishing sixth in the league. Andre Villas-Boas, who began the season as our new manager, left in March and was replaced by club legend Roberto Di Matteo, who had scored in two FA Cup finals for Chelsea as a player. He led us to the Champions League final as we came from behind to beat Napoli in the last 16, then defeated Benfica in the quarter-finals and, most impressively of all, overcame Barcelona in the semi-finals.

That was a great Barcelona team, managed by Pep Guardiola and starring Lionel Messi, Xavi and Andres Iniesta, but we managed to defend brilliantly against them. We won the home leg 1-0 thanks to a goal from Didier Drogba, then the away leg was one of the greatest games in Chelsea history.

We went 2-0 down and had our captain John Terry sent off and it looked like we would be knocked out. Then Ramires scored a brilliant chip to give us the lead on away goals just before half-time, and we sealed victory in the last few seconds of the game thanks to a breakaway goal from Fernando Torres.

THE BIG OCCASION

This was our second Champions League final, but we had lost the previous one to Manchester United in Moscow four years earlier, so Chelsea fans were desperate to make sure we came home with the trophy this time.

Our opponents this time were Bayern Munich and the final was being held in their home stadium, which meant they were hot favourites. However, Chelsea had won the FA Cup final the previous weekend and there was a feeling that it was our destiny to win this year's competition. After all, many of the players involved had been with the club for several years and had come so close to winning the Champions League in their time here. We had reached the semi-finals in 2004, 2005, 2007 and 2009, and lost the final on penalties in 2008. This time, we had to do it.

THE FINAL

 Bayern   **1**
Müller 83'

 Chelsea   **1**
Drogba 88'

Chelsea win 4-3 on penalties

It was a tense game, and it looked like Bayern Munich had won it when Thomas Muller scored with seven minutes left in the game. However, Drogba was the ultimate big-game player, and he headed in a corner from Juan Mata with one minute left to draw us level.

The game went to extra time, and Bayern won a penalty, but Petr Cech saved from his former Chelsea team-mate Arjen Robben and so the match had to be decided by a penalty shoot-out.

Our first penalty was taken by Mata and it was saved, but we recovered well. Cech saved two penalties, including one from Bayern captain Bastian Schweinsteiger, and we scored the rest of ours. Drogba scored the final penalty and we were champions of Europe for the first time!

CHAMPIONS LEAGUE
IDENTITY PARADE

Here's our starting line-up from the 2012 Champions League final. We've written a statement about each of the 11 players pictured, but can you match each one to the correct player?

| 24 | Gary **Cahill** | | 4 | David **Luiz** |

| 12 | John Mikel **Obi** | 1 | Petr **Cech** | 8 | Frank **Lampard (c)** |

| 34 | Ryan **Bertrand** | 10 | Juan **Mata** | 11 | Didier **Drogba** |

| 3 | Ashley **Cole** | 17 | Jose **Bosingwa** | 21 | Salomon **Kalou** |

1   I'm the only person in this picture who also started the 2019 Europa League final for Chelsea.

2   I was a Portuguese international who had previously won the competition while at Porto.

3   I scored the winning penalty in the shoot-out!

4   I once went six seasons between goals for Chelsea, and ended up with only six from 372 appearances.

5   I'd lost two Champions League finals with different clubs before finally lifting the trophy in 2012.

6   I have won a European final while playing for Chelsea, but I've also lost one against the Blues when I was playing for Arsenal.

7   I was named as Chelsea's Player of the Year in the year that we won the Champions League.

8   I was playing for Bolton Wanderers just a few months before the Champions League final.

9   During my six years at Chelsea I scored 60 goals for the club.

10   I became the Blues' head coach in 2019.

11   This was my first-ever game in the Champions League! No one else has ever made their debut in the competition in the final.

Answers on p63

50 YEARS OF
Blue Is The Colour

You've probably heard the song hundreds of times, but did you know the famous Chelsea anthem Blue is the Colour was recorded 50 years ago ahead of the 1972 League Cup final? Here's the story of one of the catchiest tunes in football history...

BLUES IN THE STUDIO

"Blue is the colour, football is the game, we're all together, and winning is our aim!"

There are quite a few songs that Chelsea fans love to sing along to on matchdays, but not many of them have lasted as long as Blue is the Colour, which was recorded in March 1972.

This season will mark the 50th anniversary of the beloved anthem, which was written by Daniel Boone and Rod McQueen and sung by the Chelsea players. It has been played countless times over the speakers at Stamford Bridge in the half-century since and sung by fans all around the world, as we cheer our team on through the sun and rain.

It's often the first song to be played after Chelsea win cup finals, but do you know the story behind 'Blue is the Colour'?

Peter Osgood celebrates scoring Chelsea's goal in the League Cup final at Wembley, but it ended in a 2-1 defeat to Stoke City

THE STORY OF THE SONG

The song was recorded by the team ahead of the 1972 League Cup final against Stoke City, and you can see them posing at the studio in our main image. It reached number five in the singles charts when it was released by Penny Farthing Records, but although the song was a great success, the game wasn't.

Sadly, the 1972 League Cup final ended in defeat for Chelsea. Even though legendary Blues striker Peter Osgood scored an equaliser for us just before half-time at Wembley, we ended up losing 2-1 to Stoke, who were a strong team back then. Thankfully, that game was quickly forgotten by the Blues supporters, while the song has become part of the fabric of the club.

Blue Is The Colour

THE CHELSEA FOOTBALL TEAM

REMEMBERING
THE DOC

Chelsea Football Club lost one of our most charismatic and innovative former managers when Tommy Docherty passed away at the end of 2020. He may have been in the Stamford Bridge dugout long before your time, but here are a few reasons why he'll never be forgotten...

Tough act to follow

Docherty initially came to Chelsea as a player-coach in 1961, but he was soon asked to take over from Ted Drake, who at the time was the only man to have led us to a league title, and he became only the sixth full-time manager in our history. Lesser men may have winced at that prospect, but Doc was no shrinking violet and even relegation in his first few months in the dugout didn't deter him.

Doc's Diamonds

There is little doubt over the most enduring legacy from Docherty's days in west London. Upon his appointment in 1961, the Scottish manager placed his faith in young talent, picking 19 graduates from the youth team during his first season. A few had played a part in leading us to consecutive FA Youth Cup triumphs – and some of them became huge names in our history. There's Ron Harris, our all-time leading appearance

maker; Bobby Tambling, who was our record goalscorer for almost 50 years before Frank Lampard surpassed his tally; and Peter Bonetti, who once held the club record for most clean sheets. We could go on and on...

Blue (and white) is the colour

There's something about the Chelsea kit that just works – the blue shirts and shorts, with white socks bringing it all together. Well, we've got Docherty to thank for that. Prior to his time at Chelsea, we'd always worn white shorts, but he decided blue would be a much better choice and in 1964 the change was made to the colours we still wear today.

Quick off the mark

The press absolutely loved Docherty and many of those who had the pleasure of dealing with him saw similarities when Jose Mourinho was appointed as Blues boss. As a typical jocular Scot, Docherty was never short of a quip or two – although occasionally he could be a little too close to the bone with some of his comments. He once joked that any passes by Tony Hateley, the centre-forward he signed for Chelsea for a club-record fee, should be marked "to whom it may concern" and that the striker could trap the ball further than Docherty could kick it. Ouch!

On to Wembley

Our first-ever FA Cup final at Wembley was in 1967, which meant Docherty became the first manager to lead us out at the national stadium, although we lost to Tottenham Hotspur. The image of him walking out alongside captain Ron Harris adorned the cover of the matchday programme for the first game following his passing and was one of the biggest sellers of the season, such was his popularity.

TOMMY DOCHERTY
1928-2020

Great days

The biggest triumphs of Docherty's spell as Chelsea boss saw him lead us to promotion from Division Two and lift the League Cup for the first time in our history. The former was achieved with a 7-0 win over Portsmouth on the final day, while the League Cup was secured following a win over Leicester City. Back in those days the final was played over two legs, which meant it wasn't quite the occasion it is today.

Travel Man

As well as managing the Blues, Docherty had spells with 12 other clubs – including one in Portugal and two in Australia – and took charge of his country for a year. The most famous of these jobs came with Manchester United, who he led to FA Cup glory in 1977 with a win over Liverpool.

SPOT ON!

Chelsea have had more penalty scorers in Premier League history than any other club, with 25. Here's a look at some of our best and the techniques they used, plus a chance for you to see if you can match Jorginho's tally from last season.

Technique:
Make your mind up

Success rate:

No one even comes close to Frank Lampard's 41 Premier League pens for the Blues. Super Frank would always make his mind up early and trust his impeccable shooting technique to see him through.

 DID YOU KNOW?
As of the end of the 2020/21 season, 16 players had a 100 per cent conversion rate from the penalty spot for Chelsea. After **Jimmy Floyd Hasselbaink** on 12 comes **Willian** (five), **Cesc Fabregas, Michael Ballack, Eidur Gudjohnsen** and **John Spencer** (all two), and then 10 scored the only penalty they took.

Technique:
Put your foot through it

Success rate:

Jimmy Floyd Hasselbaink scored 12 out of 12 penalties in the top flight for the Blues with his no-nonsense technique.

 DID YOU KNOW?
Spare a thought for **Lucas Piazon** and **Claude Makelele**, who both took one penalty apiece – and missed! At least Maka was able to put in the rebound from his missed effort, which was one of two Chelsea goals he scored, but Piazon left us without ever finding the back of the net for the Blues.

Technique:
Keep watching...

Success rate:

Eden Hazard had an 89 per cent conversion rate from the spot and his go-to penalty technique was to watch the keeper and then stick it in the opposite corner.

Don't try this at home!

Success rate:

★ ★ ★ ★ ★

Practice makes perfect with this unusual hop, skip and jump technique, while keeping your eyes on the keeper at all times and then sending him the wrong way. Not one for the faint-hearted, but it usually works for Jorginho...

WHERE DID JORGINHO GO?

QUIZ

Jorginho finished as our leading scorer in the 2020/21 Premier League season with seven goals, each of which came from the penalty spot. Put an x where you think he placed each one and then check the answers on p63 to see how you got on.

JUNIOR BLUES

WEEKLY
COMPETITIONS
EXCLUSIVE
PRIZES
FUN VIDEOS

FREE TO JOIN!

CHELSEAFC.COM/JUNIORBLUES

OVER LAND AND SEA

Thomas Tuchel is the first German to manage Chelsea, but he's not the only boss from overseas to have sat in the Stamford Bridge dugout. We've picked out a few of them since Ruud Gullit became the first in 1996 – your job is to match them to the correct flag.

ISRAELI

Claudio **Ranieri**

The Tinkerman, who famously led Leicester to Premier League glory in 2016, is not the only one from his country to manage Chelsea. Gianluca Vialli, Carlo Ancelotti, Antonio Conte and Maurizio Sarri also hail from this European nation.

BRAZILIAN

Jose **Mourinho**

A three-time Premier League winner with the Blues, Mourinho won the UEFA Cup and Champions League with a club from his homeland before coming to Chelsea.

ITALIAN

Guus **Hiddink**

Twice installed as interim manager at Stamford Bridge, Hiddink comes from the country who gave us Total Football and what his fellow countryman and ex-Chelsea boss Ruud Gullit called Sexy Football!

SPANISH

Avram **Grant**

Grant is the only manager from his country, where the official language is Hebrew, to lead a Premier League club. He also had spells in charge at Portsmouth and West Ham.

DUTCH

Luiz Felipe **Scolari**

Big Phil, as he's known, came to Chelsea after a stint in charge of Portugal, but that's not his home country, who he also managed twice. In fact, he won the World Cup with them in 2002!

PORTUGUESE

Rafa **Benitez**

The former Liverpool boss wasn't the most popular appointment at Chelsea, although he did go on to lead us to Europa League glory in 2013.

Answers on p63

49

CHELSEA WOMEN

It was another stellar campaign for Chelsea Women, as we lifted three domestic honours and reached the final of the Women's Champions League for the first time in the club's history.

SERIAL WINNERS

Since winning our first trophy in 2015, the Blues have been almost unstoppable when it comes to racking up domestic honours. Last season's haul of three started with the Community Shield, which was played for the first time since 2008, as we defeated Manchester City at Wembley. We then added the Continental League Cup with a 6-0 win over Bristol City at Watford's Vicarage Road, before retaining our Barclays Women's Super League title on the final day of the campaign by beating Reading 5-0. What a season!

FINAL GOTHENBURG 2021
Gamla Ullevi - 16 May
Chelsea FC Women vs FC Barcelona

EURO NEAR MISS

The 2020/21 season was almost perfect, as we also came within 90 minutes of winning the Champions League! Our run to the final was thrilling, as Ann-Katrin Berger saved two penalties against Atletico Madrid, Pernille Harder helped to see off her old club and our big rivals Wolfsburg, and then Fran Kirby edged us past Bayern Munich in an incredibly tense semi-final. Unfortunately, Barcelona were too much for us in the final in Gothenburg, but we'll be back...

KERR-BY

The numbers posted by Fran Kirby and Sam Kerr in the 2020/21 season were simply off the chart. The duo recorded more than 50 goal involvements – that's goals scored and assisted – between them in the WSL. That means they had a hand in almost three quarters of our tally! Fans quickly came up with a nickname for the most devastating partnership in the league, dubbing them 'Kerr-by'.

EMMA HAYES' BLUE AND WHITE ARMY

An incredible 10 trophies have been won during Emma Hayes' time as Chelsea manager, which began in August 2012. No one can come close to matching that tally in the WSL era, but there's more to our boss than her work on the training pitch. She's a mum to a little boy called Harry, she was part of ITV's commentary team at the European Championship last summer, and back in 2016 the Queen awarded her an MBE!

GOLDEN GIRLS

As well as all the team honours we collected throughout the season, there were individual prizes too. Kirby won the Player of the Year awards from both the Football Writers' Association and the WSL, which was a remarkable achievement considering she'd missed almost an entire year of football leading up to last term. Ann-Katrin Berger added the WSL's Golden Glove award after keeping the most clean sheets, while Kerr won the Golden Boot as the leading scorer, meaning she's now done that in England, Australia and the USA!

OLYMPIC BLUES

Jessie Fleming made history at the Tokyo Olympics, as she became the first Chelsea Women's player ever to win a gold medal. Fleming scored a penalty in the final for Canada and then successfully converted in the shoot-out to help her country past a Sweden squad containing fellow Blues Magda Eriksson, Jonna Andersson and Zecira Musovic. In all we had 11 players competing in Japan.

FAREWELL FARA

Fara Williams bowed out of the professional game with more England caps than any other player, as she represented her country a whopping 172 times! It was fitting that her final game for Reading came against Chelsea, as the midfielder started her career with the Blues, which is the club she supports.

WSL PIONEERS

It seems like only yesterday that the Women's Super League began, but April 2021 marked 10 years since the new league began. Chelsea were involved in the first-ever fixture of the competition, when we hosted Arsenal, but it wasn't really a day to remember for the Blues. We lost 1-0 and the only goal of the game was scored by Gilly Flaherty, who went on to become a Chelsea legend a few years later.

SHINING BRIGHT

Blues vice-captain Millie Bright reveals how she got into football and what has changed in the sport since the days when she aspired to become a professional at the top of the game.

Starting out

The women's game existed when I was growing up, but professional football wasn't on the cards just then. For me, I played football purely for enjoyment, just being in a team environment and around my friends. Football was a hobby. People ask me, "When did you think you'd become a pro?" and the answer is the day I signed my first professional contract! It's nice to see the game has changed and little girls can say, "I want to grow up and become a professional footballer." We're getting there.

Breaking barriers

No matter what you do in life, there's always going to be good and bad comments. People would say things like, "It's a man's game," but I think that's changed now. We've grown through that, it's made us stronger and more determined to change the game. No matter the sport, it's all equal.

Culture club

At Chelsea we've always been a team of many internationals, but even more so now, with some of the coaching staff coming from different backgrounds. It's really nice, you get to learn about their culture from back home and their experiences, the lifestyle. Getting to know one another has been super interesting, really great. Players coming from abroad have become the norm and that's not just at Chelsea, that's across the Women's Super League. It's the best league in the women's game and it's a privilege to be playing in it.

Biggest influences

I think my family. My mum and dad, my grand-dad, I think they've always believed in me, even when I was semi-professional and we didn't know I was going to become a pro. They always believed in me being a better player and enjoying the game. My coaches have also been massive. My teacher back in secondary school, Nicky Turner, she always told me I'd be a pro and I just laughed it off. She always said, "Go for what you believe in. You'll play for England one day." I thought there was no chance! It's those sorts of people who don't just say they believe in you, they show you.

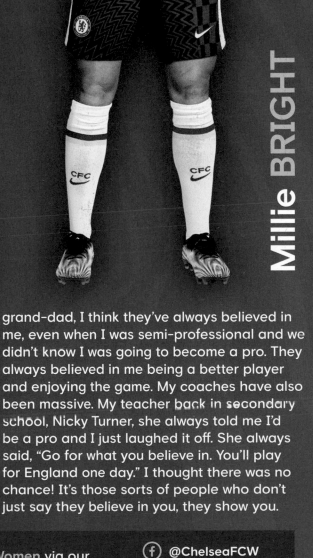

Millie BRIGHT

Make sure you keep up with all things Chelsea Women via our social media platform, which is full of behind-the-scenes access and content that you simply cannot find elsewhere.

@ChelseaFCW
@ChelseaFCW
@ChelseaFCW

SUPER, SUPER FRAN!

The 2020/21 season is one Fran Kirby won't forget in a hurry. The Chelsea Women legend enjoyed the best campaign of her career, as she won major honours both individually and collectively with her team-mates.

After almost a year out of the game with a serious illness, no one knew what to expect from Fran Kirby when she made her long-awaited return to the Chelsea Women starting line-up in August 2020. It's safe to say that not even in her wildest dreams could the Blues No. 14 have dreamed of a campaign quite like it.

She was pivotal in leading the club to the FA Women's Super League title and Continental League Cup, contributing 16 goals and 11 assists from 18 league games. She also netted six times to help us to the Champions League final for the first time, as well as overtaking Eniola Aluko as the Blues' all-time leading goalscorer.

To top it all off, she won a shedload of individual prizes, too. On top of the Millennium and Resorts Chelsea Women's Player of the Year award, she also won the WSL, Football Writers' Association and PFA Player of the Year. The latter two were also awarded to her in 2018, but this year it was all the sweeter after her struggles off the pitch.

2020/21 stats

Women's Super League

Games: **18**

Goals: **16**

Assists: **11**

UEFA Women's Champion's League

Games: **9**

Goals: **6**

Assists: **1**

Q&A

How does it feel to win these awards, particularly the PFA prize which is voted for by your fellow professionals?
It's an amazing achievement, really special. First and foremost, obviously my team-mates are amazing and without them I would have never won any of the awards or trophies that I have already. I'm really, really humbled.

Did the season go even better than you could have expected in your wildest dreams?
I never had any expectations coming into the season. I never had any expectations of playing as much as I did, never mind winning the awards and trophies! I always knew playing for this team, I would be able to win titles and trophies, but it's really special and something I definitely didn't anticipate happening.

How hard did you have to work to get back to your best level after so long out?
I've been able to take my game to another level and while everyone sees the end product, no one sees what goes on behind closed doors. I still think I have more to give. I'm always critical of my own performance and I'm always going to pick out things that I really want to improve on. At the moment I'm in a really good place and playing the best football I ever have done and I'm just glad I'm able to be a part of this team and able to show all the hard work that I've put in.

Tell us a bit about your motivation last season and what got you going.
My motivation was definitely within myself. It was to try and show myself that I could get back to a level I was proud of, and I didn't know if that was going to happen. I just said to myself, "Give it everything and see what happens." For me, it was a case of getting back into the environment, being around the girls and trying to show them I wasn't going to get left behind in any of the pre-season fitness training and that, I think, started the journey for me.

Here at Chelsea, you're part of a group that has made winning trophies habitual...
It's what we're here for. We speak about it at the beginning of every season, how much we want to win all the trophies we can. The difference now is the mentality – we're never satisfied. We don't win a trophy and think that's our job done, we win a trophy and think, "When's the next one?" That's the mentality we have in this team, in this group.

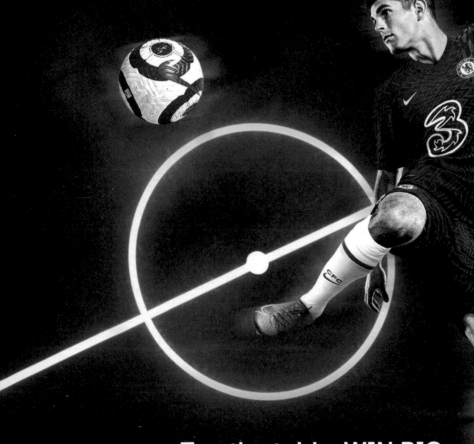

SPOT THE DIFFERENCE

See if you can spot the **SEVEN** differences!

Answers on p63

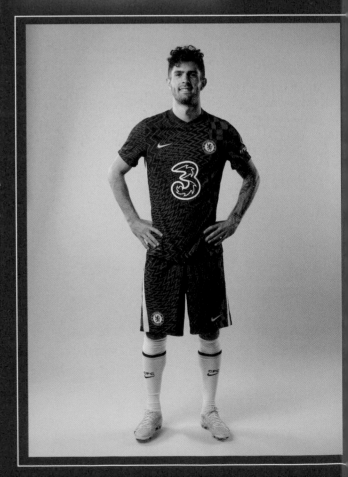

WIN... A SIGNED CHELSEA SHIRT!

You could be the proud owner of a Chelsea home shirt signed by the men's first-team squad. We have one to give away to a lucky fan who can correctly answer the question below. For your chance to be the lucky winner, get thinking and send us your answer. Good luck!

Who scored the winning goal in Chelsea's Champions League final victory over Manchester City in May 2021?

A) Mason **Mount**   **B)** Kai **Havertz**   **C)** Timo **Werner**

Entry is by email only. Only one entry per contestant. Please enter CFC SHIRT followed by either A, B or C in the subject line of an email. In the body of the email, please include your full name, address, postcode, email address, phone number and date of birth and send to: frontdesk@grangecommunications.co.uk **by Thursday 31st March 2022.**

Competition Terms and Conditions

1. The closing date for this competition is Thursday 31st March 2022 at midnight. Entries received after that time will not be counted.
2. Information on how to enter and on the prize form part of these conditions.
3. Entry is open to those residing in the UK only. If entrants are under 18, consent from a parent or guardian must be obtained and the parent or guardian must agree to these terms and conditions. If entrants are under 13, this consent must be given in writing from the parent or guardian with their full contact details.
4. This competition is not open to employees or their relatives of Chelsea Football Club. Any such entries will be invalid.
5. The start date for entries is 31st October 2021 at 4pm.
6. Entries must be strictly in accordance with these terms and conditions. Any entry not in strict accordance with these terms and conditions will be deemed to be invalid and no prize will be awarded in respect of such entry. By entering, all entrants will be deemed to accept these rules.
7. One (1) lucky winner will win a 2021/22 season signed men's football shirt.
8. The prize is non-transferable and no cash alternative will be offered. Entry is by email only. Only one entry per contestant. Please enter CFC SHIRT followed by either A, B or C in the subject line of an email. In the body of the email, please include your full name, address, postcode, email address and phone number and send to: frontdesk@ grangecommunications.co.uk by Thursday 31st March 2022.
9. The winner will be picked at random. The winner will be contacted within 72 hours of the closing date. Details of the winner can be requested after this time from the address below.
10. Entries must not be sent in through agents or third parties. No responsibility can be accepted for lost, delayed, incomplete, or for electronic entries or winning notifications that are not received or delivered. Any such entries will be deemed void.
11. The winner will have 72 hours to claim their prize once initial contact has been made by the Promoter. Failure to respond may result in forfeiture of the prize.
12. At Chelsea FC plc and our group companies, we go the extra mile to ensure that your personal information is kept secure and safe. We will not share your information with any other companies or use your data other than as necessary to administrate the competition. Once the competition is over your information will be securely destroyed. Your information will always be safeguarded under the terms and conditions of the Data Protection Act 1998 and CFC's Privacy Policy (https://www.chelseafc.com/en/footer/privacy-policy) to ensure that the information you provide is safe.
13. The Promoter reserves the right to withdraw or amend the promotion as necessary due to circumstances outside its reasonable control. The Promoter's decision on all matters is final and no correspondence will be entered into.
14. The Promoter (or any third party nominated by the Promoter) may contact the winner for promotional purposes without notice and without any fee being paid.
15. Chelsea Football Club's decision is final; no correspondence will be entered in to. Except in respect of death or personal injury resulting from any negligence of the Club, neither Chelsea Football Club nor any of its officers, employees or agents shall be responsible for (whether in tort, contract or otherwise):
- (i) any loss, damage or injury to you and/or any guest or to any property belonging to you or any guest in connection with this competition and/or the prize, resulting from any cause whatsoever;
- (ii) for any loss of profit, loss of use, loss of opportunity or any indirect, economic or consequential losses whatsoever.
16. This competition shall be governed by English law.
17. Promoter: Grange Communications Ltd, 22 Great King Street, Edinburgh EH3 6QH.

EXTRA ⏱ TIME

As you reach the end of the Chelsea Annual, you're probably wondering what's left for you to know about the Blues. Well, how about a few of our players telling you something interesting about them?

My sister Lauren plays for Chelsea as well. I'm really proud of where she's got to. We always played as a family. My older brother Josh learned from my dad and then it just passed its way down. We all used to play every day together at the park and over time we all gradually got better – it was just a case of play with the ball, play as much as you can, and learn as much as you can without any help, get a love for the game.

Reece **James**

Gaming is something I do on days off, and after games when I cannot sleep. I started very young, playing with my brother on the Playstation 2. We played FIFA 2005 and 2006. It continues now for 15 more years! FIFA 2005 was the year you could start making your own character. My brother and I built ourselves and then we played against each other and it was like a war! When I lost I got angry, some controllers were broken, so it was always very competitive even though he is seven years older than me.

Kai **Havertz**

I lived on a street that was round and there was a playing ground in the middle with a grass field and all the children on the street would play. It wasn't really a fun kickabout when it came to me as it was always very serious and I got so angry if we lost! I always played against boys, including at school in breaks and stuff. I was always doing tackles and running around. I never really thought of it as being something special, it was just natural to me because I loved to play. The boys didn't think it was weird I was with them.

Magdalena **Eriksson**

As a kid, I always loved Thierry Henry and Zinedine Zidane, so it was pretty much between the two of them as to which was my favourite. Henry was just a leader on the pitch, he scored some great goals and he really helped pull Arsenal through a lot of times during the Invincibles season. Zidane was just Zidane – what more can you say about him? He's just one of the best midfielders that ever played the game. He's not done badly as a manager, either!

Drew **Spence**

When I was young I went to Morocco a lot but after a while I was not there so often. You always play on the streets or wherever, and you don't have the things that you have in Europe because you play on sand, you play on the street but on the street you see everywhere broken things. That kind of thing makes it harder because when you fall you never know what is on the ground. I have had crazy things on the ground and cut myself open.

Hakim **Ziyech**

I love Nike trainers. Air Forces are what I wear day-to-day because they literally go with anything you wear but then also Dunks are becoming pretty common now. They're a super cool trainer so a lot of the boys are starting to get into wearing them now, myself included. I have a bit of a trainer collection and I like to keep them all looking as fresh and clean as possible. I've also got a collection of hats – baseball caps, trucker caps, beanies. Pretty much whenever I go out, unless it's a smart event where I need to do my hair, I'll always have a cap on.

Ben **Chilwell**

Playing in Spain, Italy and England has been important for me to grow and to be the man I am today. I have learned the difference between these countries, these cultures, these types of football. I have played different styles in each team, too.

Marcos **Alonso**

I used to do judo as a kid and my coach said if I'd pursued it like I had football then I'd have probably gone quite far. I obviously chose football, but that was mainly because I was the only girl at the judo club I went to, so I was always fighting against boys and they got a lot bigger, whereas I stopped growing at the age of 10! I also really enjoyed being part of a team environment, rather than just being on my own.

Fran **Kirby**

I have always been someone who is discreet, an introvert, but this is not something that takes away from my confidence and doing what I like. When I play football, it's what I like. It's what we train for, what we think about every day. When we are on the pitch it's a chance to do well and fight for what you want. That's why on the pitch I like doing my best and trying to help the team. I enjoy that.

N'Golo **Kante**

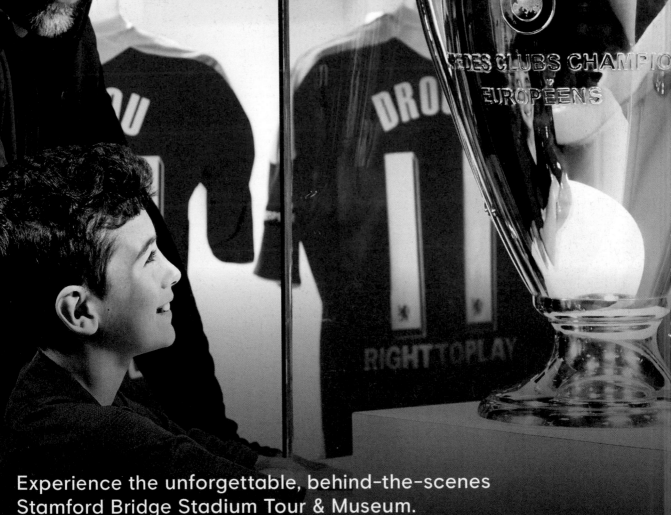

Chelsea FC
Stadium Tours
& Museum

Experience the unforgettable, behind-the-scenes
Stamford Bridge Stadium Tour & Museum.

Children's Birthday Tours are available.

Search: CFC Tours

THE PRIDE OF LONDON